Opposites

for kids age 1-3

by Dayna Martin

e ENGAGE BOOKS

Mailing address
PO BOX 4608
Main Station Terminal
349 West Georgia Street
Vancouver, BC
Canada, V6B 4A1

www.engagebooks.ca

Written & compiled by: Dayna Martin
Edited & designed by: A.R. Roumanis
Photos supplied by: Shutterstock

FIRST EDITION / FIRST PRINTING

LIBRARY AND ARCHIVES CANADA CATALOGUING IN PUBLICATION

Martin, Dayna, 1983–, author
    Opposites for kids age 1-3 / written by Dayna Martin ; edited by A.R. Roumanis.

(Engage early readers : children's learning books)
Issued in print and electronic formats.
ISBN 978-1-77226-075-5 (paperback). –
ISBN 978-1-77226-076-2 (bound). –
ISBN 978-1-77226-077-9 (pdf). –
ISBN 978-1-77226-078-6 (epub). –
ISBN 978-1-77226-079-3 (kindle)

1. English language – Synonyms and antonyms – Juvenile literature.
I. Roumanis, A. R., editor
II. Title.

PE1591.M365 2015   J428.1   C2015-903410-8
                                          C2015-903411-6

Opposites

for kids age 1-3

Engage Early Readers

Children's Learning Books

by Dayna Martin

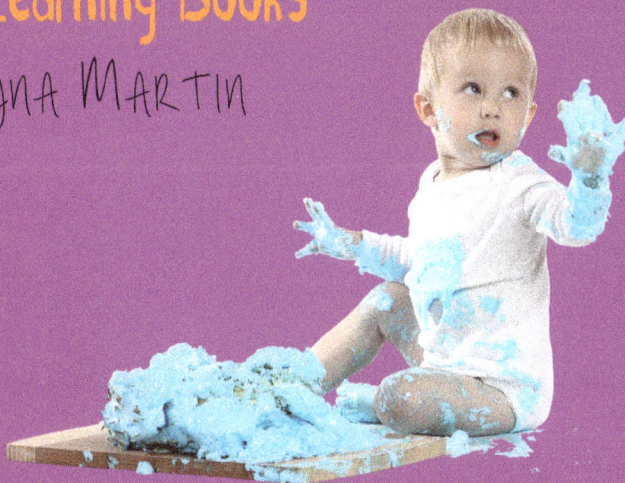

ENGAGE BOOKS / VANCOUVER

3

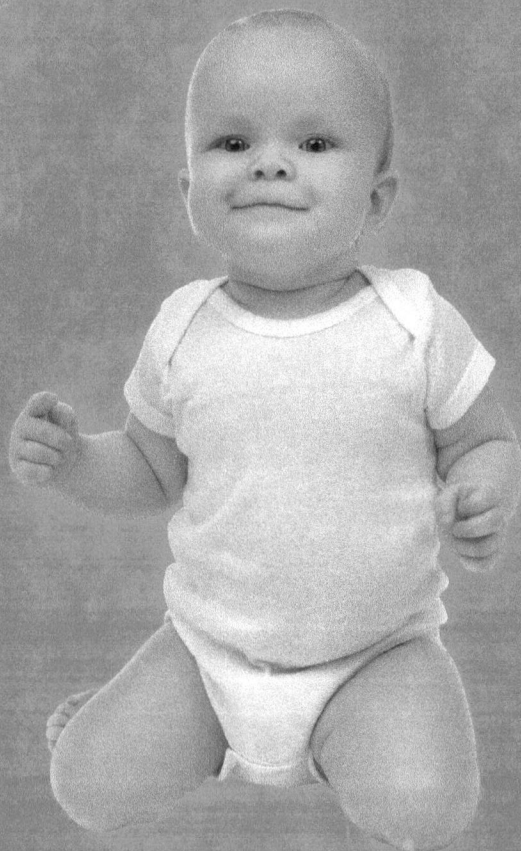

Up   Down

4

In

Out

5

Big   Small

6

Clean

Dirty

Empty   Full

8

Safe   Dangerous

Hot   Cold

Wet

Dry

Long   **Short**

12

Slow   Fast

13

Few

Many

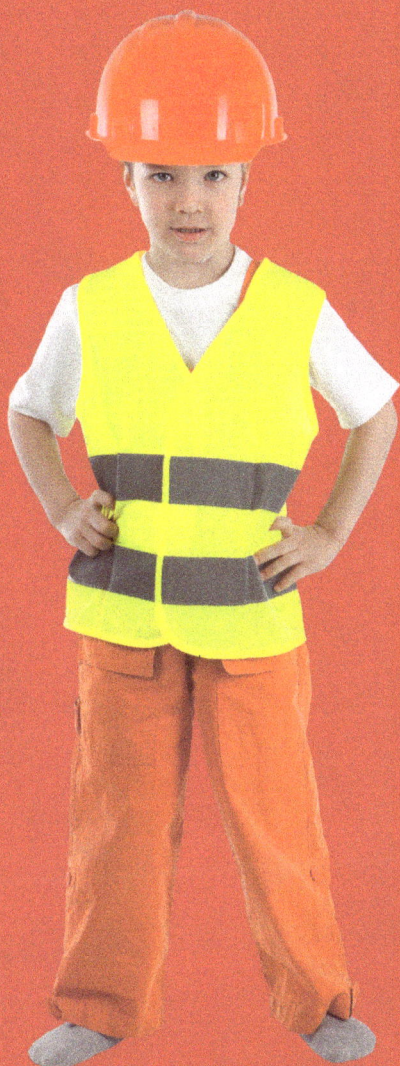 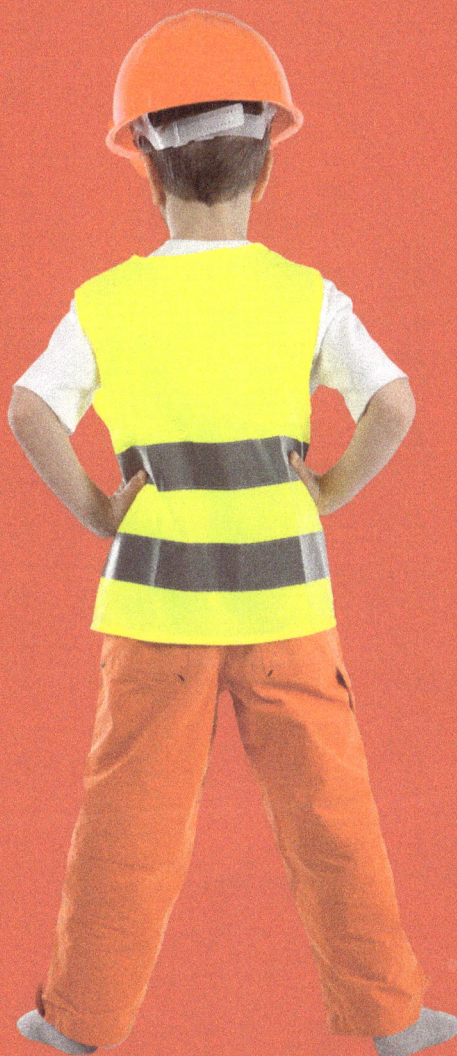

Front   Back

15

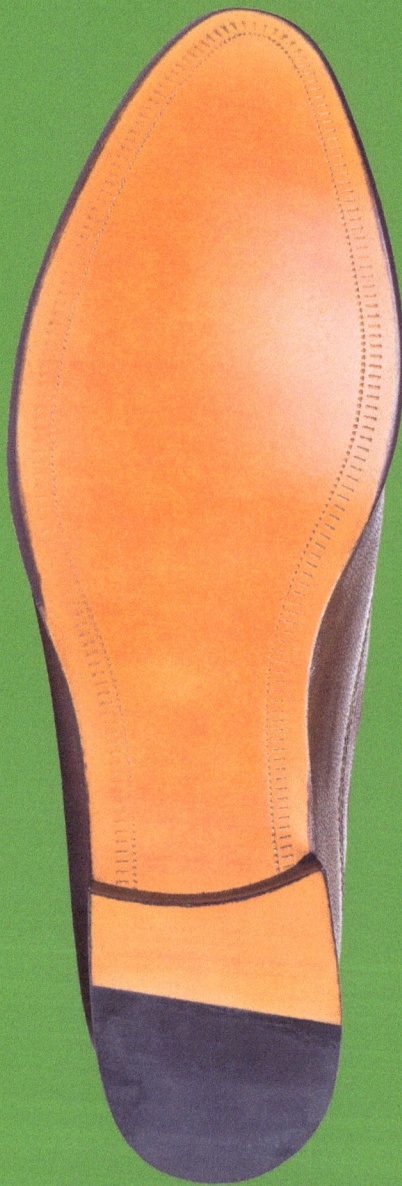

Smooth   **Rough**

16

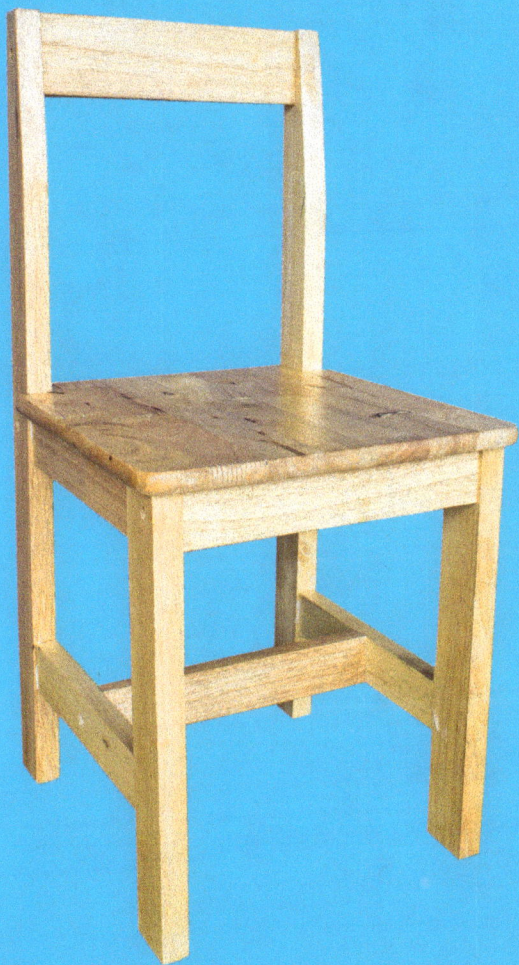

Hard **Soft**

17

Heavy

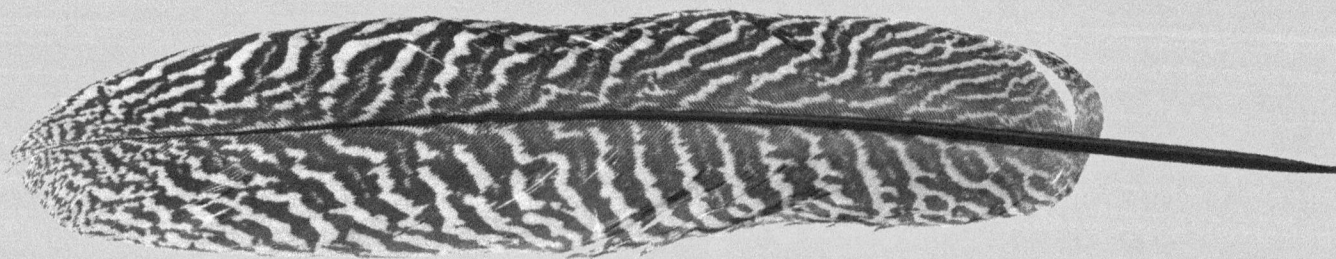

Light

18

Sit   Stand

19

Above

Below

Loose

Tight

21

New

Old

Young

Old

23

On   Off

Open

Closed

25

Tall   Short

26

Far

Near

27

Asleep   **Awake**

Dark   **Light**

Thick

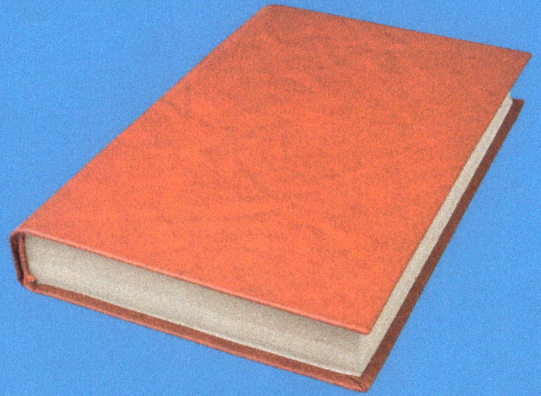

Thin

Happy

Sad

29

Opposites activity

Do you remember what these opposites are called? Can you find **heavy/light, in/out, hot/cold,** and **hard/soft**? Match the opposites below.

Answer: in

Answer: heavy

Answer: hot

Answer: hard

Answer: cold

Answer: soft

30

Answer: out

Answer: light

Colors for Kids
age 1-3

Yellow Fish · Orange Flower · Purple Eggplant · White Bear · Red Fire Hydrant · Blue Hat · Pink Pig · Green Lego

ABCs for Kids
age 1-3

Fox · Lion · Vulture · Tiger · Bear · Rabbit · Dog · Cat

Actions for Kids
age 1-3

Eat · Jump · Crawl · Brush · Wave · Kick · Swim · Ride

Sizes for Kids
age 1-3

Small · Medium · Large · Small · Medium · Large · Small · Medium · Large · Medium · Large · Small · Medium · Small · Large · Medium · Large · Medium · Small · Large · Small

Numbers for Kids
age 1-3

4 Raspberries · 7 Rubber Ducks · 2 Cars · 8 Presents · 5 Cups · 1 Bowl · 6 Balloons · 3 Pickles

Emotions for Kids
age 1-3

Bored · Silly · Proud · Shy · Brave · Grumpy · Shock · Fear

Shapes for Kids
age 1-3

Starfish · Clock · Leaf · Chalkboard · Door · Rings · Cracker · Pizza

Sounds for Kids
age 1-3

Ribbit · Moo · Vroom · Flush · Clap · Ring · Roar · Cock-a-doodle-doo

Sports for Kids
age 1-3

Badminton · Basketball · Baseball · Volleyball · Soccer · Golf · Tennis

www.ingramcontent.com/pod-product-compliance
Lightning Source LLC
Chambersburg PA
CBHW051310020426
42331CB00020B/3498